Edited by
Alan C. Whitmore

Hymns We Love to Sing

111 Favorites

Large Print

WoodLake

Editor: Alan C. Whitmore
Cover Design: Lois Huey-Heck
Design and Layout: Lois Huey-Heck and Alan C. Whitmore
Consulting Art Director: Robert MacDonald
Permissions: Lindy Jones

We thank the owners and copyright holders for their cooperation in making the publication of this book possible. Specific credit will be found with each hymn.

A number of the hymns included in this selection are traditional, anonymous, or in public domain – that is, any copyright that once existed has expired. For these hymns, no specific credit has been given. We caution users of this book against assuming that they may make use of any version of these hymns without requiring permission; while the words, melody, and harmony may be free of copyright restrictions, the physical presentation on the page is copyright by the publisher.

We have made every effort to track all owners and copyright holders. If we have omitted any legitimate owners and copyright holders, we sincerely apologize. We will include the appropriate credit in future editions and reprints of the book, and will make royalty payments on the same basis as was offered to other copyright holders.

BNC CERTIFIED GOLD BIBLIOGRAPHIC DATA 2014-15

WoodLake is an imprint of Wood Lake Publishing, Inc. Wood Lake Publishing acknowledges the financial support of the Government of Canada through the Canada Book Fund (CBF) for its publishing activities. Wood Lake Publishing also acknowledges the financial support of the Province of British Columbia through the Book Publishing Tax Credit.

At Wood Lake Publishing, we practise what we publish, being guided by a concern for fairness, justice, and equal opportunity in all of our relationships with employees and customers. Wood Lake Publishing is committed to caring for the environment and all creation. Wood Lake Publishing recycles, reuses, and encourages readers to do the same. Resources are printed on 100% post-consumer recycled paper and more environmentally friendly groundwood papers (newsprint), whenever possible. A percentage of all profit is donated to charitable organizations.

Canadian Cataloguing in Publication Data
Main entry under title:
Hymns we love to sing [text (large print)]
ISBN 978-1-55145-151-0
Hymns, English—Texts. 2. Large type books.
BV350.H96 1995 245'.21 C95-910759-2

Copyright © 1995 by Wood Lake Publishing Inc.
All rights reserved. No part of this publication may be reproduced, stored in a retrieval system, or transmitted, by any means, electronic, mechanical, photocopying, recording, or otherwise, without the prior written permission of the copyright holder or the publisher, Wood Lake Books, Inc., as appropriate.Published by Wood Lake Books, Inc.

Published by Woodlake
An imprint of Wood Lake Publishing Inc.
485 Beaver Lake Road, Kelowna, BC, Canada, V4V 1S5
www.woodlakebooks.com
250.766.2778

Printing 10 9 8
Printed in Canada

Introduction

Hymns We Love to Sing resulted from numerous requests of parish clergy and health care professionals. They asked for a collection of familiar hymns which could be used anywhere a large-print, light-weight format was needed: in congregations, hospitals, care facilities, funeral homes, and for personal use.

The major challenge was assembling the largest number of hymns in a limited space. The collection needed to be familiar, intergenerational, and cover a wide thematic range. While there is no thematic index, the hymns are grouped in a thematic way. There are also hymns for each major season of the church year.

Where possible, the layout follows the guidelines of the Large Print Publishing Program of the National Library of Canada.

We hope that *Hymns We Love to Sing* will encourage the continued singing of hymns by all members of the family of God and give users another means to praise our Creator.

Dedication

This book is dedicated to Bert and Mary Whitmore, who taught me and countless others the hymns we love to sing.

Acknowledgments

The contents of this book of hymns is due to the input of many people. Thanks go to Barbara Barnett, Sharon Beckstead, George Black, Michael Bloss, Howard Box, Lesley Clare, Mark Gibson, Marilyn Hunter, Wayne Irwin, Flora Litt, Janice and Richard Olfert, Robert Pletsch, Ken Powers, Donald Schmidt, Helene Scott, Mike Skibinski, John Smallman, and Rae E. Whitney, for their interest and support.

Many thanks also go to Jim Taylor and David Cleary, of Wood Lake Books, for their encouragement and support.

Foreword

It would be impossible to thank everyone whose contribution made this large print hymn book a reality. One group however, does stand out in my mind. They are the patients who, over the years, made up the ecumenical worshipping community at the Queen Elizabeth Hospital, Toronto.

They were Christians of all stripes. From time to time they were joined by persons from other faith groups, who like them were responding to the need to be engaged with others in an act of worship.

I learned from them. They taught me that hymns that were meaningful to them were the ones that helped them feel connected. Some hymns had rhythm and movement; some created a sense of peace. All helped them feel as if they belonged and that they were involved with Someone or something greater than themselves. These hymns strengthened the weary soul and enabled people of various beliefs to bind together as humankind before their Lord, however that was understood by them.

Some of these people were too handi-capped to sing, but a word mouthed here and there, a tapping hand or foot moving in time to the music, spoke of their in-volvement. Occasionally a tear trickled down a face. Amidst the many losses they were experiencing, these people were supported by the words and music of hymns capable of inspiring hope and nourishing the need to commune with their God.

We hope that the hymns that are found within this book are just those kind of hymns for you.

Rev. Marilyn Hunter
Manager, Chaplaincy
Queen Elizabeth Hospital
July 26, 1995

Come Thou Long-Expected Jesus

1. Come, thou long-expected Jesus,
    born to set thy people free:
    from our fears and sins release us,
    let us find our rest in thee.

2. Israel's strength and consolation,
    hope of all the earth thou art,
    dear desire of every nation,
    joy of every longing heart.

3. Born thy people to deliver;
    born a child and yet a King;
    born to reign in us for ever;
    now thy gracious kingdom bring.

4. By thine own eternal Spirit
    rule in all our hearts alone;
    by thine all-sufficient merit
    raise us to thy glorious throne.

Meter: 8 7 8 7

Words: Charles Wesley, 1707–1788

2   **Away in a Manger**

1. Away in a manger,
   no crib for a bed,
   the little Lord Jesus
   laid down his sweet head.
   The stars in the bright sky
   looked down where he lay,
   the little Lord Jesus
   asleep on the hay.

2. The cattle are lowing,
   the baby awakes,
   but little Lord Jesus
   no crying he makes.
   I love you, Lord Jesus;
   look down from the sky,
   and stay by my side
   until morning is nigh.

3. Be near me, Lord Jesus,
   I ask you to stay
   close by me for ever,
   and love me, I pray.
   Bless all the dear children
   in your tender care,
   and fit us for heaven,
   to live with you there.

Meter: 11 11 11 11

Author unknown

Good Christians All, Rejoice 3

1. Good Christians all, rejoice
    with heart and soul and voice!
    Give ye heed to what we say:
    News! News!
    Jesus Christ is born today.
    Ox and ass before him bow,
    and he is in the manger now,
    Christ is born today!

2. Good Christians all, rejoice
    with heart and soul and voice!
    Now ye hear of endless bliss:
    Joy! Joy!
    Jesus Christ was born for this.
    He hath oped the heavenly door,
    and we are blessed for evermore.
    Christ was born for this!

3. Good Christians all, rejoice
    with heart and soul and voice!
    Now ye need not fear the grave:
    Peace! Peace!
    Jesus Christ was born to save,
    calls you one and calls you all
    to gain his everlasting hall.
    Christ was born to save!

Meter: irregular

Words: John Mason Neale, 1818–1866

4 O Come, All Ye Faithful

1. O come, all ye faithful,
      joyful and triumphant,
   O come ye,
      O come ye to Bethlehem;
   come and behold him,
      born the King of angels:

   Refrain:
   O come, let us adore him,
   Christ the Lord.

2. Sing, choirs of angels,
      sing in exultation,
   sing, all ye citizens
      of heaven above;
   glory to God in the highest:

3. Yea, Lord, we greet thee,
      born this happy morning;
   Jesus, to thee be glory given;
   word of the Father,
      now in flesh appearing:

Meter: irregular

Words: John Francis Wade, c. 1711–1786
tr. Frederick Oakeley, 1802–1880

Joy to the World 5

1. Joy to the world, the Lord is come!
   let earth receive her King;
   let every heart prepare him room,
   and heaven and nature sing.

2. Joy to the world, the Savior reigns!
   let all their songs employ;
   while fields and floods, rocks, hills,
        and plains
   repeat the sounding joy.

3. No more let sins and sorrows grow,
   nor thorns infest the ground;
   he comes to make his blessings flow
   far as the curse is found.

4. He rules the world with truth
        and grace,
   and makes the nations prove
   the glories of his righteousness,
   and wonders of his love.

Meter: CM with Repeat

Words: Isaac Watts, 1674–1748

6 The Huron Carol

1. 'Twas in the moon of wintertime,
   when all the birds had fled,
   that mighty Gitchi Manitou
   sent angel choirs instead;
   before their light
       the stars grew dim,
   and wondering hunters
       heard the hymn:
   Jesus your King is born,
       Jesus is born,
   in excelsis gloria.

2. Within a lodge of broken bark
   the tender babe was found,
   a ragged robe of rabbit skin
   enwrapped his beauty round;
   but as the hunter braves
       drew nigh,
   the angel song rang
       loud and high:
   Jesus your King is born,
       Jesus is born,
   in excelsis gloria.

3. O children of the forest free,
    O sons of Manitou,
    the holy child of earth
        and heaven
    is born today for you.
    Come, kneel before
        the radiant boy,
    who brings you beauty,
        peace and joy:
    Jesus your King is born,
        Jesus is born,
    in excelsis gloria.

Meter: irregular

Words: Jean de Brébeuf, 1593–1649
tr. Jesse Edgar Middleton, 1872–1960

7 Silent Night

1. Silent night! holy night!
   All is calm, all is bright
   round yon virgin
      mother and child.
   Holy infant so tender and mild,
   sleep in heavenly peace!

2. Silent night! holy night!
   Shepherds quake at the sight:
   glories stream
      from heaven afar,
   heavenly hosts sing Alleluia,
   Christ, the Savior, is born!

3. Silent night! holy night!
   Son of God, love's pure light
   radiant beams
      from thy holy face,
   with the dawn
      of redeeming grace,
   Jesus, Lord, at thy birth.

Meter: irregular

Words: Joseph Mohr, 1792–1848
tr. Jane Montgomery Campbell, 1817–1878 and others

When I Survey the Wondrous Cross 8

1. When I survey the wondrous cross
   on which the Prince of glory died,
   my richest gain I count but loss,
   and pour contempt on all my pride.

2. Forbid it, Lord, that I should boast
   save in the death of Christ, my God:
   all the vain things that charm
      me most,
   I sacrifice them to his blood.

3. See from his head, his hands,
      his feet,
   sorrow and love flow mingled down!
   Did e'er such love and sorrow meet,
   or thorns compose so rich a crown?

4. Were the whole realm of
      nature mine,
   that were a present far too small:
   love so amazing, so divine,
   demands my soul, my life, my all.

Meter: 8 8 8 8

Words: Isaac Watts, 1674–1748

9   Lord of the Dance

1.   I danced in the morning
      when the world was begun,
and I danced in the moon
      and the stars and the sun;
and I came down from heaven
      and I danced on the earth—
at Bethlehem I had my birth.

Refrain:
Dance then wherever
      you may be;
I am the Lord of the Dance,
      said he;
I'll lead you all
      wherever you may be,
I will lead you all in the dance,
      said he.

2.   I danced for the scribe
      and the pharisee,
but they would not dance
      and they wouldn't follow me;
I danced for the fishermen,
      for James and John;
they came with me
      and the dance went on.

3. I danced on the Sabbath
   and I cured the lame;
the holy people
   said it was a shame;
they whipped and they stripped
   and they hung me high,
and they left me there
   on a cross to die.

4. I danced on a Friday
   when the sky turned black—
it's hard to dance
   with the devil on your back;
they buried my body
   and they thought I'd gone—
but I am the dance
   and I still go on.

5. They cut me down
   and I leap up high:
I am the life
   that'll never, never die;
I'll live in you
   if you'll live in me—
I am the Lord of the Dance,
   said he.

Meter: irregular

Words: Sydney Carter, 1915–

10 There Is a Green Hill Far Away

1. There is a green hill far away,
   outside a city wall,
   where the dear Lord was crucified
   who died to save us all.

2. We may not know, we cannot tell,
   what pains he had to bear;
   but we believe it was for us
   he hung and suffered there.

3. He died that we might be forgiven,
   he died to make us good,
   that we might go at last to heaven,
   saved by his precious blood.

4. There was no other good enough
   to pay the price of sin;
   he only could unlock the gate
   of heaven, and let us in.

5. O dearly, dearly has he loved,
   and we must love him too,
   and trust in his redeeming blood,
   and try his works to do.

Meter: 8 6 8 6

Words: Cecil Frances Alexander, 1818–1895

Were You There? 11

1. Were you there when
   they crucified my Lord?
   Were you there when
   they crucified my Lord?

   Refrain:
   Oh! Sometimes
   it causes me to tremble,
   Were you there when
   they crucified my Lord?

2. Were you there when
   they nailed him to the tree?

3. Were you there when
   they pierced him in the side?

4. Were you there when
   they laid him in the tomb?

Meter: irregular

African-American Spiritual

12 Jesus Christ Is Risen Today

1. Jesus Christ is risen today,
      Alleluia!
   our triumphant holy day,
      Alleluia!
   who did once, upon the cross,
      Alleluia!
   suffer to redeem our loss.
      Alleluia!

2. Hymns of praise then let us sing
   unto Christ our heavenly King,
   who endured the cross and grave,
   sinners to redeem and save.

3. But the pains which he endured
   our salvation have procured;
   now above the sky he's King,
   where the angels ever sing.

4. Sing we to our God above
   praise eternal as his love;
   praise him, all ye heavenly host,
   Father, Son, and Holy Ghost.

Meter: 7 7 7 7 and Alleluia

Words: Lyra Davidica, 1708 and others

Ev'ry Morning Is Easter Morning   13

Refrain:
Ev'ry morning is Easter morning
    from now on!
Ev'ry day's resurrection day,
    the past is over and gone!

1. Goodbye guilt, goodbye fear,
        good riddance!
    Hello, Lord, Hello, sun!
    I am one of the Easter People!
    My new life has begun!

2. Daily news is so bad it seems the
    Good News seldom gets heard.
    Get it straight from
        the Easter People!
    God's in charge spread the word!

3. Yesterday I was bored and lonely;
    But today look and see!
    I belong to the Easter People!
    Life's exciting to me!

    Ev'ry morning...

Meter: irregular

Words: Richard Avery and Donald Marsh
Copyright © 1972 by Hope Publishing Co., Carol Stream,
IL 60188. All rights reserved. Used by permission.

14 Thine Is the Glory

1. Thine is the glory,
       risen, conquering Son:
   endless is the victory
       thou o'er death hast won.
   Angels in bright raiment
       rolled the stone away,
   kept the folded grave clothes
       where the body lay.
   Thine is the glory,
       risen, conquering Son:
   endless is the victory
       thou o'er death hast won.

2. Lo, Jesus meets us,
       risen from the tomb!
   Lovingly he greets us,
       scatters fear and gloom.
   Let his church with gladness
       hymns of triumph sing,
   for her Lord now liveth:
       death has lost its sting.
   Thine is the glory,
       risen, conquering Son:
   endless is the victory
       thou o'er death hast won.

3. No more we doubt thee,
   glorious Prince of life;
life is nought without thee:
   aid us in our strife;
make us more than conquerors,
   through thy deathless love;
bring us safe through Jordan
   to thy home above.
Thine is the glory,
   risen, conquering Son:
endless is the victory
   thou o'er death hast won.

Meter: 5 5 6 5 6 5 6 5 and Refrain

Words: Edmond Louis Budry, 1854–1932
tr. Richard Birch Hoyle, 1875–1939

15 The Strife Is O'er

1. The strife is o'er, the battle done;
   now is the victor's triumph won;
   O let the song of praise be sung,
   Alleluia.

2. Death's mightiest powers
         have done their worst,
   and Jesus hath his foes dispersed;
   let shouts of praise
         and joy outburst,
   Alleluia.

3. He closed the ancient gates of hell,
   the bars from heaven's high
         portals fell;
   let songs of praise his triumph tell,
   Alleluia.

4. Lord, by the stripes
         which wounded thee,
   from death's dread sting
         thy servants free,
   that we may live, and sing to thee,
   Alleluia.

Meter: 8 8 8 and Alleluia

Words: from the Latin 17th century
tr. Francis Pott, 1832–1909

Lift High the Cross 16

Refrain:
Lift high the cross,
    the love of Christ proclaim
till all the world
    adore his sacred name.

1. Come, brethren, follow
    where our Captain trod,
our King victorious,
    Christ the Son of God.

2. Led on their way
    by this triumphant sign,
the hosts of God
    in conquering ranks combine.

3. O Lord, once lifted
    on the glorious tree,
as thou hast promised,
    draw men unto thee.

4. So shall our song
    of triumph ever be
praise to the Crucified
    for victory.

Meter: 10 10 10 10

Words: George William Kitchin, 1827–1912 and
Michael Robert Newbolt, 1874–1956

17 The Old Rugged Cross

1. On a hill far away
   stood an old rugged cross,
the emblem of suffering and shame;
and I love that old cross
   where the dearest and best
for a world of lost sinners was slain.

Refrain:
So I'll cherish the old rugged cross,
till my trophies at last I lay down;
I will cling to the old rugged cross,
and exchange it some day
   for a crown.

2. O that old rugged cross,
   so despised by the world,
has a wondrous attraction for me;
for the dear Lamb of God
   left his glory above
to bear it to dark Calvary.

3. To the old rugged cross
   I will ever be true,
its shame and reproach gladly bear;
then he'll call me some day
   to my home far away,
where his glory forever I'll share.

Meter: irregular with Refrain
Words: George Bennard, 1913

Crown Him with Many Crowns

18

1. Crown him with many crowns,
   the Lamb upon his throne:
   hark, how the heavenly anthem
        drowns
   all music but its own!
   Awake, my soul, and sing
   of him who died for thee,
   and hail him as thy matchless King
   through all eternity.

2. Crown him the Lord of life,
   who triumphed o'er the grave,
   and rose victorious in the strife
   for those he came to save.
   His glories now we sing
   who died and rose on high,
   who died eternal life to bring,
   and lives that death may die.

3. Crown him the Lord of love;
   behold his hands and side,
   rich wounds yet visible above,
   in beauty glorified.
   All hail, Redeemer, hail!
   for thou hast died for me;
   thy praise shall never, never fail
   throughout eternity.

Meter: 6 6 8 6 D

Words: M. Bridges, 1800–1894 & G. Thring, 1823–1903

19 Spirit, Spirit of Gentleness

Refrain:
Spirit, Spirit of gentleness,
blow thro' the wilderness
    calling and free,
Spirit, Spirit of restlessness,
stir me from placidness,
    Wind, Wind on the sea.

1. You moved on the waters,
    you called to the deep,
then you coaxed up the mountains
    from the valleys of sleep;
and over the aeons
    you called to each thing:
wake from your slumbers
    and rise on your wings.

2. You swept thro' the desert,
    you stung with the sand,
and you goaded your people
    with a law and a land;
and when they were blinded
    with their idols and lies,
then you spoke thro' your prophets
    to open their eyes.

3. You sang in a stable,
        you cried from a hill,
    then you whispered in silence
        when the whole world was still;
    and down in the city
        you called once again,
    when you blew thro' your people
        on the rush of the wind.

4. You call from tomorrow,
        you break ancient schemes,
    from the bondage of sorrow
        the captives dream dreams;
    our women see visions,
        our men clear their eyes,
    with bold new decisions
        your people arise.

Meter: irregular

Words: James K. Manley, 1978

20 Spirit of God, Descend upon My Heart

1. Spirit of God,
         descend upon my heart;
    wean it from earth;
         through all its pulses move;
    stoop to my weakness,
         mighty as thou art,
    and make me love thee
         as I ought to love.

2. I ask no dream,
         no prophet ecstasies,
    no sudden rending
         of the veil of clay,
    no angel visitant,
         no opening skies;
    but take the dimness
         of my soul away.

3. Teach me to love thee
         as thine angels love,
    one holy passion
         filling all my frame;
    the kindling of the heaven-
         descended Dove,
    my heart an altar,
         and thy love the flame.

Meter: 10 10 10 10

Words: George Croly, 1867

Spirit of the Living God 21

1. Spirit of the living God,
    fall afresh on me.
Spirit of the living God,
    fall afresh on me.
Melt me, mold me,
    fill me, use me.
Spirit of the living God,
    fall afresh on me.

2. Spirit of the living God,
    move among us all;
make us one in heart and mind,
    make us one in love:
humble, caring,
    selfless, sharing.
Spirit of the living God,
    fill our lives with love!

Meter: 7 5 7 5 8 7 5

Words: st. 1 Daniel Iverson, st. 2 Michael Baughen
st. 1 copyright © 1935, 1963 Birdwing Music.
Admin. by EMI Christian Music Publishing.
All rights reserved. Used by permission.
st. 2 copyright © 1982 by Hope Publishing Co.,
Carol Stream, IL 60188. All rights reserved. Used by permission.

22 Breathe on Me, Breath of God

1. Breathe on me, Breath of God,
   fill me with life anew,
   that I may love what thou dost love,
   and do what thou wouldst do.

2. Breathe on me, Breath of God,
   until my heart is pure,
   until with thee I will one will,
   to do and to endure.

3. Breathe on me, Breath of God,
   till I am wholly thine,
   till all this earthly part of me
   glows with thy fire divine.

4. Breathe on me, Breath of God,
   so shall I never die,
   but live with thee the perfect life
   of thine eternity.

Meter: SM

Words: Edwin Hatch, 1878

Come, Ye Thankful People, Come — 23

1. Come, ye thankful people, come,
   raise the song of harvest-home!
   All is safely gathered in,
   ere the winter storms begin;
   God, our maker, doth provide
   for our wants to be supplied:
   come to God's own temple, come,
   raise the song of harvest-home!

2. All the world is God's own field,
   fruit unto his praise to yield;
   wheat and tares together sown,
   unto joy or sorrow grown;
   first the blade, and then the ear,
   then the full corn shall appear:
   Lord of harvest, grant that we
   wholesome grain and pure may be.

3. Even so, Lord, quickly come
   to thy final harvest-home!
   Gather thou thy people in,
   free from sorrow, free from sin;
   there for ever purified,
   in thy presence to abide:
   come, with all thine angels, come,
   raise the glorious harvest-home.

Meter: 7 7 7 7 D

Words: Henry Alford, 1810–1871

24 For the Fruit of All Creation

1. For the fruit of all creation,
   thanks be to God.
   For the gifts to ev'ry nation,
   thanks be to God.
   For the ploughing, sowing, reaping,
   silent growth while we are sleeping,
   future needs in earth's safe keeping,
   thanks be to God.

2. In the true reward of labour,
   God's will is done.
   In the help we give our neighbour,
   God's will is done.
   In our worldwide task of caring
   for the hungry and despairing,
   in the harvests we are sharing,
   God's will is done.

3. For the harvests of the Spirit,
   thanks be to God.
   For the good we all inherit,
   thanks be to God.
   For the wonders that astound us,
   for the truths that still confound us,
   most of all that love has found us,
   thanks be to God.

Meter: 8 4 8 4 8 8 8 4

Words: Fred Pratt Green, 1970

Now Thank We All Our God 25

1. Now thank we all our God,
    with heart, and hands, and voices,
    who wondrous things hath done,
    in whom his world rejoices;
    who from our mother's arms
    hath blessed us on our way
    with countless gifts of love,
    and still is ours today.

2. O may this bounteous God
    through all our life be near us,
    with ever joyful hearts
    and blessed peace to cheer us,
    and keep us in his grace,
    and guide us when perplexed,
    and free us from all ills
    in this world and the next.

3. All praise and thanks to God
    the Father now be given,
    the Son, and him who reigns
    with them in highest heaven,
    the one eternal God,
    whom heaven and earth adore;
    for thus it was, is now,
    and shall be evermore.

Meter: 6 7 6 7 6 6 6 6

Words: Martin Rinckart, 1586–1649
tr. Catherine Winkworth, 1827–1878

26 Great Is Thy Faithfulness

1. Great is thy faithfulness,
      O God our Father!
   There is no shadow
      of turning with thee;
   thou changest not,
      thy compassions they fail not;
   as thou hast been
      thou forever wilt be.

   Refrain:
   Great is thy faithfulness,
      great is thy faithfulness,
   morning by morning
      new mercies I see;
   all I have needed
      thy hand hath provided—
   great is thy faithfulness,
      Lord, unto me!

2. Summer and winter
      · and springtime and harvest,
   sun, moon and stars
      in their courses above,
   join with all nature
      in manifold witness
   to thy great faithfulness,
      mercy and love.

3. Pardon for sin
    and a peace that endureth,
thine own dear presence
    to cheer and to guide,
strength for today
    and bright hope for tomorrow
wondrous the portion
    thy blessings provide.

Meter: 11 10 11 10 with Refrain

Words: T. O. Chisholm, 1866–1960
Copyright © 1923. Renewal 1951 by Hope Publishing Co.,
Carol Stream, IL 60188. All rights reserved. Used by permission.

27 One Bread, One Body

Refrain:
One bread, one body,
  one Lord of all,
one cup of blessing
  which we bless.
And we, though many,
  throughout the earth,
we are one body
  in this one Lord.

1. Gentile or Jew,
     servant or free,
   woman or man, no more.

2. Many the gifts,
     many the works,
   one in the Lord of all.

3. Grain for the fields,
     scattered and grown,
   gathered to one, for all.

Meter: irregular

Words: John Foley, SJ, 1978
Copyright © 1978 John B. Foley, SJ and New Dawn Music,
Portland, OR 97213. All rights reserved. Used with permission.

Let Us Break Bread 28

1. Let us break bread together
      on our knees,
    let us break bread together
      on our knees.
    When I fall down on my knees
    with my face to the rising sun,
    Oh, Lord, have mercy on me.

2. Let us drink wine together
      on our knees,
    let us drink wine together
      on our knees.
    When I fall down on my knees
    with my face to the rising sun,
    Oh, Lord, have mercy on me.

3. Let us praise God together
      on our knees,
    let us praise God together
      on our knees.
    When I fall down on my knees
    with my face to the rising sun,
    Oh, Lord, have mercy on me.

Meter: 10 10 with Refrain

African-American Spiritual

29   For All the Saints

1. For all the saints
    who from their labors rest,
 who thee by faith
    before the world confessed,
 thy name, O Jesus,
    be for ever blest.
 Alleluia!

2. But lo, there breaks
    a yet more glorious day—
 the saints triumphant
    rise in bright array:
 the King of glory
    passes on his way.
 Alleluia!

3. From earth's wide bounds,
    from ocean's farthest coast,
 through gates of pearl
    streams in the countless host,
 singing to Father,
    Son, and Holy Ghost.
 Alleluia!

Meter: 10 10 10 4

Words: William Walsham How, 1823–1897

All Things Bright and Beautiful 30

Refrain:
All things bright and beautiful,
all creatures great and small,
all things wise and wonderful:
the Lord God made them all.

1. Each little flower that opens,
   each little bird that sings,
   God made their glowing colors,
   and made their tiny wings.

2. The purple-headed mountains,
   the river running by,
   the sunset and the morning
   that brightens up the sky.

3. The cold wind in the winter,
   the pleasant summer sun,
   the ripe fruits in the garden:
   God made them every one.

4. God gave us eyes to see them,
   and lips that we might tell
   how great is God Almighty,
   who has made all things well.

Meter: 7 6 7 6 with Refrain

Words: Cecil Frances Alexander, 1848

31 As Comes the Breath of Spring

1. As comes the breath of spring,
   with light, and mirth, and song,
   so does God's Spirit bring
   new days, brave, free and strong.
   You come with thrill of life
   to chase hence winter's breath,
   to hush to peace the strife
   of sin that ends in death.

2. You come like dawning day,
   with flaming truth and love,
   to chase all glooms away,
   to brace our wills to prove
   how wise, how good to choose
   the truth and its brave fight;
   to prize it, win or lose,
   and live on God's delight.

3. You come like songs at morn
   that fill the earth with joy,
   till we in Christ new-born
   new strength in praise employ.
   You come to rouse the heart
   from drifting to despair,
   thro' high hope to impart
   life, with an ampler air.

Meter: 6 6 6 6 D

Words: David L. Ritchie, 1930, rev.

Morning Has Broken 32

1. Morning has broken
       like the first morning,
    blackbird has spoken
       like the first bird.
    Praise for the singing!
       Praise for the morning!
    Praise for them, springing
       fresh from the Word!

2. Sweet the rain's new fall
       sunlit from heaven,
    like the first dew fall
       on the first grass.
    Praise for the sweetness
       of the wet garden,
    sprung in completeness
       where God's feet pass.

3. Ours is the sunlight!
       Ours is the morning
    born of the one light
       Eden saw play!
    Praise with elation,
       praise ev'ry morning,
    God's recreation
       of the new day!

Meter: 5 5 5 4 D

Words: Eleanor Farjeon, 1931
Words copyright © David Higham Associates. Used by permission.

33 When Morning Gilds the Skies

1. When morning gilds the skies,
   my heart awak'ning cries:
   may Jesus Christ be praised!
   When ev'ning shadows fall,
   this rings my curfew call:
   may Jesus Christ be praised!

2. To God the Word on high
   the hosts of angels cry:
   may Jesus Christ be praised!
   Let mortals too, upraise
   their voice in hymns of praise:
   may Jesus Christ be praised!

3. Let all of human kind
   in this their concord find:
   may Jesus Christ be praised!
   Let all the earth around
   ring joyous with the sound:
   may Jesus Christ be praised!

4. Be this while life is mine,
   my canticle divine:
   may Jesus Christ be praised!
   Be this th'eternal song,
   thro'all the ages long:
   may Jesus Christ be praised!

Meter: 6 6 6 6 6 6
Words: German, 19th C.
tr. E. Caswell, 1854, R. Bridges, 1899, rev.

For the Beauty of the Earth 34

1. For the beauty of the earth,
   for the glory of the skies,
   for the love which from our birth
   over and around us lies;

   Refrain:
   Lord of all, to thee we raise
   this our hymn of grateful praise.

2. For the beauty of each hour
   of the day and of the night,
   hill and vale, and tree and flower,
   sun and moon, and stars of light;

3. For the joy of human love,
   brother, sister, parent, child,
   friends on earth and friends above,
   for all gentle thoughts and mild;

4. For thyself, best Gift Divine,
   to the world so freely given,
   for that great, great love of thine,
   peace on earth, and joy in heaven:

Meter: 7 7 7 7 7 7

Words: Folliot S. Pierpoint, 1864

35 Rejoice, the Lord Is King

1. Rejoice, the Lord is King;
   your Lord and King adore;
   rejoice, give thanks and sing
   and triumph evermore:
   lift up your heart, lift up your voice:
   Rejoice; again I say, Rejoice.

2. Jesus the Saviour reigns,
   the God of truth and love;
   when he had purged our stains,
   he took his seat above:
   lift up your heart...

3. He sits at God's right hand
   till all his foes submit,
   and bow to his command,
   and fall beneath his feet:
   lift up your heart...

4. Rejoice in glorious hope;
   Jesus, the Judge, shall come
   and take his servants up
   to their eternal home:
   we soon shall hear
        the archangel's voice;
   the trump of God shall sound, Rejoice.

Meter: 6 6 6 6 8 8

Words: Charles Wesley, 1707–1788

This Is God's Wondrous World

36

1. This is God's wondrous world,
   and to my listening ears
   all nature sings, and round me rings
   the music of the spheres.
   This is God's wondrous world;
   I rest me in the thought
   of rocks and trees, of skies and seas,
   whose hand the wonders wrought.

2. This is God's wondrous world:
   the birds their carols raise,
   the morning light, the lily white,
   declare their Maker's praise.
   This is God's wondrous world:
   God shines in all that's fair;
   in the rustling grass or mountain pass,
   God's voice speaks everywhere.

3. This is God's wondrous world:
   O let me ne'er forget
   that though the wrong seems oft
       so strong,
   God is the ruler yet.
   This is God's wondrous world:
   the battle is not done;
   Jesus, who died, shall be satisfied,
   and earth and heaven be one.

Meter: 6 6 8 6 D
Words: Maltbie Davenport Babcock, 1901, rev.

37   **This Is the Day**

1.   This is the day,
      that the Lord has made;
we will rejoice,
      and be glad in it.
This is the day
      that the Lord has made,
we will rejoice
      and be glad in it.
This is the day,
      that the Lord has made.

2.   Open to us,
      the gates of God;
we will go in,
      and praise the Lord.
Open to us
      the gates of God,
we will go in
      and praise the Lord.
Open to us,
      the gates of God.

3. You are our God,
  we will praise your name;
 we will give thanks,
  for your faithfulness.
 You are our God,
  we will praise your name,
 we will give thanks
  for your faithfulness.
 You are our God,
  we will praise your name.

4. This is the day,
  that the Lord has made;
 we will rejoice,
  and be glad in it.
 This is the day
  that the Lord has made,
 we will rejoice
  and be glad in it.
 This is the day,
  that the Lord has made.

Meter: irregular

Words: vs. 1 Source unknown, vs. 2&3,
Songs for a Gospel People.
Words copyright © vs. 2 & 3 *Songs for a Gospel People.*
Used by permission.

38 All Hail the Power of Jesus' Name

1. All hail the power of Jesus' name!
   Let angels prostrate fall;
   bring forth the royal diadem
   to crown him, Lord of all.

2. Hail him, ye heirs of David's line,
   whom David Lord did call,
   the God incarnate, Man divine,
   and crown him, Lord of all.

3. Let every tongue and every tribe,
   responsive to the call,
   to him all majesty ascribe,
   and crown him, Lord of all.

4. O that, with yonder sacred throng,
   we at his feet may fall,
   join in the everlasting song,
   and crown him, Lord of all!

Meter: 8 6 8 6 and repeat

Words: Edward Perronet, 1726–1792 and others

All People That on Earth Do Dwell 39

1. All people that on earth do dwell,
   sing to the Lord with cheerful voice,
   him serve with mirth, his praise
       forth tell;
   come ye before him and rejoice.

2. Know that the Lord is God indeed;
   without our aid he did us make;
   we are his folk, he doth us feed,
   and for his sheep he doth us take.

3. O enter then his gates with praise,
   approach with joy his courts unto;
   praise, laud, and bless his name
       always,
   for it is seemly so to do.

4. For why, the Lord our God is good;
   his mercy is for ever sure;
   his truth at all times firmly stood,
   and shall from age to age endure.

Meter: 8 8 8 8

Words: attr. to William Kethe, C. 1530–1594

40 Christ Is Made the Sure Foundation

1. Christ is made the sure foundation,
   Christ the head and cornerstone
   chosen of the Lord, and precious,
   binding all the church in one,
   holy Zion's help for ever,
   and her confidence alone.

2. To this temple where we call thee
   come, O Lord of hosts, today;
   with thy wonted loving-kindness
   hear thy servants as they pray,
   and thy fullest benediction
   shed within its walls alway.

3. Here vouchsafe to all thy servants
   what they ask of thee to gain,
   what they gain from thee for ever
   with the blessed to retain,
   and hereafter in thy glory
   evermore with thee to reign.

4. Laud and honor to the Father,
   laud and honor to the Son,
   laud and honor to the Spirit,
   ever three and ever one,
   one in might, and one in glory,
   while unending ages run.

Meter: 8 7 8 7 8 7

Words: 7th C. Latin, tr. John M. Neale, 1818–1866

Glorious Things of Thee Are Spoken 41

1. Glorious things of thee are spoken,
   Zion, city of our God;
   God, whose word cannot be broken,
   formed thee for his own abode.
   On the Rock of Ages founded,
   what can shake thy sure repose?
   With salvation's walls surrounded,
   thou mayst smile at all thy foes.

2. See, the streams of living waters,
   springing from eternal love,
   well supply thy sons and daughters,
   and all fear of want remove.
   Who can faint while such a river
   ever will their thirst assuage?
   Grace which like the Lord, the giver,
   never fails from age to age.

3. Blest inhabitants of Zion,
   washed in our Redeemer's blood;
   Jesus, whom our souls rely on,
   makes us monarchs, priest to God.
   Us, by his great love, he raises,
   rulers over self to reign,
   and as priests his solemn praises
   we for thankful offering bring.

Meter: 8 7 8 7 D

Words: John Newton, 1725–1807

42 Holy, Holy, Holy, Lord God Almighty

1. Holy, holy, holy,
       Lord God almighty!
   early in the morning
       our song shall rise to thee;
   holy, holy, holy,
       merciful and mighty,
   God in three persons,
       blessed Trinity!

2. Holy, holy, holy!
       all the saints adore thee,
   casting down their golden crowns
       around the glassy sea,
   cherubim and seraphim
       falling down before thee,
   which wert, and art,
       and evermore shalt be.

3. Holy, holy, holy,
       Lord God almighty!
   All thy works shall praise thy name
       in earth and sky and sea;
   holy, holy, holy,
       merciful and mighty,
   God in three persons,
       blessed Trinity!

Meter: irregular

Words: Reginald Heber, 1783–1826

Immortal, Invisible, God Only Wise 43

1. Immortal, invisible,
     God only wise,
  in light inaccessible
     hid from our eyes,
  most blessed, most glorious,
     the Ancient of days,
  almighty, victorious,
     thy great name we praise.

2. To all life thou givest,
     to both great and small;
  in all life thou livest,
     the true life of all;
  we blossom and flourish
     as leaves on the tree,
  and wither and perish—
     but nought changeth thee.

3. Great Father of glory,
     pure Father of light,
  thine angels adore thee,
     all veiling their sight;
  all laud we would render:
     O help us to see
  'tis only the splendor
     of light hideth thee.

Meter: 11 11 11 11

Words: Walter Chalmers Smith, 1824–1908

44 How Great Thou Art

1. O Lord my God!
      when I in awesome wonder
   consider all the worlds
      thy hands have made,
   I see the stars,
      I hear the rolling thunder,
   thy power throughout
      the universe displayed.

   Refrain:
   Then sings my soul,
      my Savior God to thee;
   how great thou art,
      how great thou art!

2. When through the woods
      and forest glades I wander,
   and hear the birds
      sing sweetly in the trees;
   when I look down
      from lofty mountain grandeur
   and hear the brook,
      and feel the gentle breeze;

3. And when I think that God,
    his Son not sparing,
sent him to die,
    I scarce can take it in;
that on the cross,
    my burden gladly bearing,
he bled and died
    to take away my sin;

4. When Christ shall come
    with shout of acclamation
and take me home,
    what joy shall fill my heart.
Then I shall bow
    in humble adoration,
and there proclaim,
    my God, how great thou art!

Meter: irregular with refrain

45 Joyful, Joyful We Adore Thee

1. Joyful, joyful we adore thee,
   God of glory, Lord of love;
   hearts unfold like flowers before thee,
   opening to the sun above.
   Melt the clouds of sin and sadness,
   drive the dark of doubt away;
   giver of immortal gladness,
   fill us with the light of day.

2. All thy works with joy surround thee,
   earth and heaven reflect thy rays;
   stars and angels sing around thee,
   center of unbroken praise.
   Field and forest, vale and mountain,
   flowery meadow, flashing sea,
   chanting bird and flowing fountain,
   call us to rejoice in thee.

3. Thou art giving and forgiving,
   ever blessing, ever blest,
   well-spring of the joy of living,
   ocean depth of happy rest!
   Thou our Father, Christ our Brother,
   all who live in love are thine;
   teach us how to love each other,
   lift us to the joy divine.

Meter: 8 7 8 7 D

Words: Henry van Dyke, 1852–1933 and compilers

Praise, My Soul, the King of Heaven 46

1. Praise, my soul, the King of heaven;
   to his feet thy tribute bring;
   ransomed, healed, restored, forgiven,
   who like thee his praise should sing?
   Praise him, praise him, alleluia,
   praise the everlasting King.

2. Praise him for his grace and favor
   to our fathers in distress;
   praise him, still the same for ever,
   slow to chide and swift to bless;
   praise him...glorious in his faithfulness.

3. Frail as summer's flower we flourish;
   blows the wind and it is gone;
   but, while mortals rise and perish,
   God endures unchanging on:
   praise him...praise the high eternal one.

4. Angels, help us to adore him,
   ye behold him face to face;
   sun and moon bow down before him:
   dwellers all in time and space,
   praise him...praise with us the God of
   grace.

Meter: 8 7 8 7 8 7

Words: Henry Francis Lyte, 1793–1847

47 Praise to the Lord, the Almighty

1. Praise to the Lord, the Almighty,
       the King of creation;
   O my soul, praise him,
       for he is thy health and salvation:
   all ye who hear,
       brothers and sisters draw near,
   praise him in glad adoration.

2. Praise to the Lord, who o'er all things
       so wondrously reigneth,
   shelters thee under his wings,
       yea, so gently sustaineth:
   hast thou not seen
       what thy entreaties have been
   granted in what he ordaineth?

3. Praise to the Lord! O let all
       that is in me adore him!
   All that hath life and breath
       come now with praises before him!
   Let the Amen
       sound from his people again:
   gladly for aye we adore him.

Meter 14 14 4 7 8

Words: Joachim Neander, 1650–1680
tr. Catherine Winkworth, 1827–1878 and others

The Church's One Foundation 48

1. The church's one foundation
    is Jesus Christ her Lord:
    she is his new creation
    by water and the word;
    from heaven he came and sought her
    to be his holy bride;
    with his own blood he bought her,
    and for her life he died.

2. Elect from every nation,
    yet one o'er all the earth,
    her charter of salvation
    one Lord, one faith, one birth,
    one holy name she blesses,
    partakes one holy food,
    and to one hope she presses
    with every grace endued.

3. Yet she on earth hath union
    with God the three in one,
    and mystic sweet communion
    with those whose rest is won.
    O happy ones and holy!
    Lord, give us grace that we,
    like them, the meek and lowly,
    on high may dwell with thee.

Meter: 7 6 7 6 D

Words: Samuel John Stone, 1839–1900

49 Blessed Assurance

1. Blessed assurance, Jesus is mine!
   O what a foretaste of glory divine!
   Heir of salvation, purchase of God,
   born of his Spirit, washed in his blood.

   Refrain:
   This is my story, this is my song,
   praising my Savior all the day long;
   this is my story, this is my song,
   praising my Savior all the day long.

2. Perfect submission, perfect delight,
   visions of rapture now burst
         on my sight;
   angels descending bring from above
   echoes of mercy, whispers of love.

3. Perfect submission, all is at rest;
   I in my Savior am happy and blest,
   watching and waiting, looking above,
   filled with his goodness,
         lost in his love.

Meter: 9 10 9 9 with refrain

Words: Fanny J. Crosby, 1873

Guide Me, O Thou Great Jehovah 50

1. Guide me, O thou great Jehovah,
   pilgrim through this barren land.
   I am weak, but thou art mighty;
   hold me with thy powerful hand.
   Bread of heaven,
   feed me till I want no more.

2. Open now the crystal fountain
   whence the healing stream
           doth flow;
   let the fiery cloudy pillar
   lead me all my journey through.
   Strong deliverer,
   be thou still my strength
           and shield.

3. When I tread the verge of Jordan,
   bid my anxious fears subside;
   death of death,
           and hell's destruction,
   land me safe on Canaan's side:
   songs of praises
   I will ever give to thee.

Meter: 8 7 8 7 8 7 and repeat

Words: William Williams, 1716–1791
tr. Peter Williams, 1723–1796

51 I Need Thee Every Hour

1. I need thee every hour,
      most gracious Lord;
   no tender voice like thine
      can peace afford.

   Refrain:
   I need thee, O I need thee;
      every hour I need thee;
   O bless me now, my Savior,
      I come to thee.

2. I need thee every hour,
      in joy or pain;
   come quickly and abide,
      or life is vain.

3. I need thee every hour;
      teach me thy will;
   and thy rich promises
      in me fulfill.

4. I need thee every hour,
      most Holy One;
   O make me thine indeed,
      thou blessed Son.

Meter: 6 4 6 4 with refrain

Words: Annie S. Hawks, 1872

Jesus Loves Me   52

1. Jesus loves me, this I know,
and the Bible tells me so;
little ones to him belong,
in his love we shall be strong.

   Refrain:
   Yes, Jesus loves me,
   yes, Jesus loves me,
   yes, Jesus loves me,
   the Bible tells me so.

2. Jesus loves me, this I know,
as he loved so long ago,
taking children on his knee,
saying, 'Let them come to me.'

3. Jesus loves me still today,
walking with me on my way,
wanting as a friend to give
light and love to all who live.

Meter: 7 7 7 7 and refrain

Words: Anna Bartlett Warner, C. 1822–1915 and
David Rutherford McGuire, 1929–1971
Revised words copyright © David Rutherford McGuire.
Used by permission of Cherie McGuire.

53 Nearer, My God, to Thee

1. Nearer, my God, to thee,
   nearer to thee!
   Even though it be a cross
   that raiseth me,
   still all my song would be
   'Nearer, my God, to thee,
   nearer, my God, to thee,
   nearer to thee!'

2. Though, like the wanderer,
   the sun gone down,
   darkness be over me,
   my rest a stone,
   yet in my dreams I'd be
   nearer, my God, to thee,
   nearer, my God, to thee,
   nearer to thee.

3. There let the way appear
   steps unto heaven;
   all that thou sendest me
   in mercy given;
   angels to beckon me
   nearer, my God, to thee,
   nearer, my God, to thee,
   nearer to thee.

4. Then with my waking thoughts
      bright with thy praise,
   out of my stony griefs
      Bethel I'll raise,
   so by my woes to be
   nearer, my God, to thee,
   nearer, my God, to thee,
   nearer to thee.

5. Or if on joyful wing
      cleaving the sky,
   sun, moon, and stars forgot,
      upwards I fly,
   still all my song shall be
   'Nearer, my God, to thee,
   nearer, my God, to thee,
   nearer to thee!'

Meter: 6 4 6 4 6 6 4

Words: Sarah Flower Adams, 1805–1848

Walk with Me   54

Walk with me,
   I will walk with you,
and build the land
   that God has planned
where love shines through.

Meter: 3 5 8 4

Words: John S. Rice, 1988

55   My Faith Looks Up to Thee

1. My faith looks up to thee,
        thou Lamb of Calvary,
        Savior divine!
   Now hear me while I pray,
   take all my guilt away,
   O let me from this day
        be wholly thine!

2. May thy rich grace impart
        strength to my fainting heart,
        my zeal inspire!
   As thou hast died for me,
   O may my love to thee
   pure, warm, and changeless be,
        a living fire!

3. While life's dark maze I tread,
        and griefs around me spread,
        be thou my guide;
   bid darkness turn to day,
   wipe sorrow's tears away,
   nor let me ever stray
        from thee aside.

Meter: 6 6 4 6 6 6 4

Words: Ray Palmer, 1875

Rock of Ages, Cleft for Me 56

1. Rock of Ages, cleft for me,
   let me hide myself in thee;
   let the water and the blood,
   from thy wounded side which flowed,
   be of sin the double cure;
   save from wrath and make me pure.

2. Not the labors of my hands
   can fulfill thy law's demands;
   could my zeal no respite know,
   could my tears forever flow,
   all for sin could not atone;
   thou must save, and thou alone.

3. While I draw this fleeting breath,
   when mine eyes shall close in death,
   when I soar to worlds unknown,
   see thee on thy judgment throne,
   Rock of Ages, cleft for me,
   let me hide myself in thee.

Meter: 7 7 7 7 7 7

Words: Augustus M. Toplady, 1776

57 The Lord's My Shepherd

1. The Lord's my shepherd, I'll not want:
   he makes me down to lie
   in pastures green; he leadeth me
   the quiet waters by.

2. My soul he doth restore again,
   and me to walk doth make
   within the paths of righteousness,
   even for his own name's sake.

3. Yea, though I walk through death's
        dark vale,
   yet will I fear no ill;
   for thou art with me, and thy rod
   and staff me comfort still.

4. My table thou hast furnished
   in presence of my foes;
   my head thou dost with oil anoint,
   and my cup overflows.

5. Goodness and mercy all my life
   shall surely follow me,
   and in God's house for evermore
   my dwelling-place shall be.

Meter: CM

Words: Scottish Psalter, 1650

Hymn of Promise   58

1. In the bulb there is a flower;
   in the seed, an apple tree;
   in cocoons, a hidden promise:
   butterflies will soon be free!
   In the cold and snow of winter
   there's a spring that waits to be,
   unrevealed until its season,
   something God alone can see.

2. There's a song in every silence,
   seeking word and melody;
   there's a dawn in every darkness,
   bringing hope to you and me.
   From the past will come the future;
   what it holds, a mystery,
   unrevealed until its season,
   something God alone can see.

3. In our end is our beginning;
   in our time, infinity;
   in our doubt there is believing;
   in our life, eternity.
   In our death, a resurrection;
   at the last, a victory,
   unrevealed until its season,
   something God alone can see.

Meter: 8 7 8 7 D

Words: Natalie Sleeth, 1986
Copyright © 1986 by Hope Publishing Co., Carol Stream,
IL 60188. All rights reserved. Used by permission.

59 O God, Our Help in Ages Past

1. O God, our help in ages past,
   our hope for years to come,
   our shelter from the stormy blast,
   and our eternal home.

2. Under the shadow of thy throne
   thy saints have dwelt secure;
   sufficient is thine arm alone,
   and our defence is sure.

3. Before the hills in order stood,
   or earth received her frame,
   from everlasting thou art God,
   to endless years the same.

4. A thousand ages in thy sight
   are like an evening gone,
   short as the watch that
       ends the night
   before the rising sun.

5. O God, our help in ages past,
   our hope for years to come,
   be thou our guard while troubles last,
   and our eternal home.

Meter: CM

Words: Isaac Watts, 1674–1748

Shall We Gather at the River

1. Shall we gather at the river,
   where bright angel feet have trod,
   with its crystal tide forever
   flowing by the throne of God?

   Refrain:
   Yes, we'll gather at the river,
   the beautiful, the beautiful river;
   gather with the saints at the river
   that flows by the throne of God.

2. On the margin of the river,
   washing up its silver spray,
   we will walk and worship ever,
   all the happy golden day.

3. Ere we reach the shining river,
   lay we every burden down;
   grace our spirits will deliver,
   and provide a robe and crown.

4. Soon we'll reach the shining river,
   soon our pilgrimage will cease;
   soon our happy hearts will quiver
   with the melody of peace.

Meter: 8 7 8 7 with refrain

Words: Robert Lowry, 1864

61 Will Your Anchor Hold?

1. Will your anchor hold
       in the storms of life?
   When the clouds unfold
       their wings of strife,
   when the strong tides lift
       and the cables strain,
   will your anchor drift
       or firm remain?

   Refrain:
   We have an anchor
       that keeps the soul
   steadfast and sure
       while the billows roll,
   fastened to the rock
       which cannot move,
   grounded firm and deep
       in the Savior's love.

2. It will surely hold
       in the straits of fear,
   when the breakers tell
       that the reef is near;
   though the tempest rave
       and the wild winds blow,
   not an angry wave
       shall our bark o'erflow.

3. It will surely hold
 in the floods of death,
when the waters cold chill
 our latest breath;
on the rising tide
 it can never fail
while our hope abide
 within the veil.

4. When our eyes behold,
 through the gathering night,
the city of gold,
 our harbor bright,
we shall anchor fast
 by the heavenly shore,
with the storms all past
 for evermore.

Meter: 10 10 10 10 and refrain

Words: Priscilla Jane Owens, 1829–1899

62   Unto the Hills

1. Unto the hills around do I lift up
     my longing eyes:
   O whence for me shall my
     salvation come, from whence arise?
   From God the Lord
     doth come my certain aid,
   from God the Lord who heaven
     and earth hath made.

2. He will not suffer that thy foot
     be moved: safe shalt thou be.
   No careless slumber shall his
     eyelids close who keepeth thee.
   Behold, he sleepeth not,
     he slumbereth ne'er,
   who keepeth Israel
     in his holy care.

3. From every evil shall he keep
     thy soul, from every sin:
   Jehovah shall preserve thy going
     out, thy coming in.
   Above thee watching,
     he whom we adore
   shall keep thee henceforth,
     yea, for evermore.

Meter: 10 4 10 4 10 10

Words: John Campbell, 1845–1914

Come, Let Us Sing of a Wonderful Love 63

1. Come, let us sing
        of a wonderful love,
    tender and true,
    out of the heart of the Father above,
    streaming to me and to you:
    wonderful love,
    dwells in the heart
        of the Father above.

2. Jesus the Savior this gospel to tell
    joyfully came—
    came with the helpless
        and hopeless to dwell,
    sharing their sorrow and shame,
    seeking the lost,
    saving, redeeming
        at measureless cost.

3. Come to my heart,
        O thou wonderful love!
    Come and abide,
    lifting my life till it rises above
    envy and falsehood and pride:
    seeking to be,
    lowly and humble, a learner of thee.

Meter: 10 8 10 7 8 10

Words: Robert Walmsley, 1831–1905

64 In the Garden

1. I come to the garden alone
   while the dew is still on the roses,
   and the voice I hear falling on my ear,
   the Son of God discloses.

   Refrain:
   And he walks with me,
   and he talks with me,
   and he tells me I am his own;
   and the joy we share
       as we tarry there,
   none other has ever known.

2. He speaks, and the sound
       of his voice
   is so sweet the birds hush
       their singing,
   and the melody that he gave to me
   within my heart is ringing.

3. I'd stay in the garden with him
   though the night around me
       be falling,
   but he bids me go;
       thru the voice of woe
   his voice to me is calling.

   Meter: 8 9 5 5 7 with refrain
   Words: C. Austin Miles, 1913

In Loving Partnership 65

1. In loving partnership we come
   seeking, O God, your will to do.
   Our prayers and actions
       now receive,
   we freely offer them to you.

2. We are the hands and feet of Christ
   serving, by grace, each other's need.
   We dare to risk and sacrifice
   with truthful word and faithful deed.

3. Loving community we seek;
   your hope and strength
       within us move.
   The poor and rich,
       the strong and weak
   are brought together in your love.

4. In loving partnership, O God,
   help us your future to proclaim.
   Justice and peace be our desire
   we humbly pray in Jesus' name.

Meter: 8 8 8 8

Words: Jim Strathdee, 1983
Copyright © 1983 by Desert Flower Music,
Carmichael, CA 95609.
Used by permission.

66 Love Divine, All Loves Excelling

1. Love divine, all loves excelling,
   joy of heaven to earth come down,
   fix in us thy humble dwelling,
   all thy faithful mercies crown.
   Jesus, thou art all compassion,
   pure, unbounded love thou art;
   visit us with thy salvation,
   enter every trembling heart.

2. Come, almighty to deliver;
   let us all thy grace receive;
   suddenly return, and never,
   never more thy temples leave.
   Thee we would be always blessing,
   serve thee as thy hosts above,
   pray, and praise thee, without ceasing,
   glory in thy perfect love.

3. Finish, then, thy new creation;
   pure and spotless let us be;
   let us see thy great salvation
   perfectly restored in thee,
   changed from glory into glory,
   till in heaven we take our place,
   till we cast our crowns before thee,
   lost in wonder, love, and praise.

Meter: 8 7 8 7 D

Words: Charles Wesley, 1707–1788

O Love That Wilt Not Let Me Go   67

1. O Love that wilt not let me go,
   I rest my weary soul in thee;
   I give thee back the life I owe,
   that in thine ocean depths its flow
      may richer, fuller be.

2. O Light that followest all my way,
   I yield my flick'ring torch to thee;
   my heart restores its borrowed ray,
   that in thy sunshine's blaze its day
      may brighter, fairer be.

3. O Joy that seekest me thro' pain,
   I cannot close my heart to thee;
   I trace the rainbow thro' the rain
   and feel the promise is not vain
      that morn shall tearless be.

4. O Cross that liftest up my head,
   I dare not ask to fly from thee;
   I lay in dust life's glory dead
   and from the ground there
      blossoms red
      life that shall endless be.

Meter: 8 8 8 8 6

Words: George Matheson, 1882

68 I Love to Tell the Story

1. I love to tell the story
        of unseen things above,
    of Jesus and his glory,
        of Jesus and his love.
    I love to tell the story,
        because I know 'tis true;
    it satisfies my longings
        as nothing else can do.

    Refrain:
    I love to tell the story,
        'twill be my theme in glory,
    to tell the old, old story
        of Jesus and his love.

2. I love to tell the story;
        more wonderful it seems
    than all the golden fancies
        of all our golden dreams.
    I love to tell the story,
        it did so much for me;
    and that is just the reason
        I tell it now to thee.

3. I love to tell the story;
    'tis pleasant to repeat
what seems, each time I tell it,
    more wonderfully sweet.
I love to tell the story,
    for some have never heard
the message of salvation
    from God's own holy Word.

4. I love to tell the story,
    for those who know it best
seem hungering and thirsting
    to hear it like the rest.
And when, in scenes of glory,
    I sing the new, new song,
'twill be the old, old story
    that I have loved so long.

Meter: 7 6 7 6 D with refrain

Words: Katherine Hankey, C. 1868

69 The Gift of Love

1. Though I may speak
      with bravest fire,
   and have the gift
      to all inspire,
   and have not love,
      my words are vain,
   as sounding brass,
      and hopeless gain.

2. Though I may give
      all I possess,
   and striving so
      my love profess,
   but not be given
      by love within,
   the profit soon
      turns strangely thin.

3. Come, Spirit, come,
      our hearts control,
   our spirits long
      to be made whole.
   Let inward love
      guide every deed;
   by this we worship,
      and are freed.

Meter 8 8 8 8

Words: Hal Hopson, 1972

Teach Me, God, to Wonder

1. Teach me, God, to wonder,
    teach me, God, to see;
    let your world of beauty
    capture me.

    Refrain:
    Praise to you be given,
    love for you be lived,
    life be celebrated,
    joy you give.

2. Let me, God, be open,
    let me loving be;
    let your world of people
    speak to me.

3. Let me, God, be ready,
    let me be awake,
    in your world of loving
    my place take.

4. Teach me, God, to know you,
    hear you when you speak,
    see you in my neighbor
    when we meet.

Meter: 6 5 6 3 with refrain

71 Tell Me the Stories of Jesus

1. Tell me the stories of Jesus
        I love to hear,
   things I would ask him to tell me
        if he were here;
   scenes by the wayside,
        tales of the sea,
   stories of Jesus, tell them to me.

2. First let me hear how the children
        stood round his knee,
   and I shall fancy his blessing
        resting on me:
   words full of kindness,
        deeds full of grace,
   all in the love-light of Jesus' face.

3. Into the city I'd follow
        the children's band,
   waving a branch of the palm tree
        high in my hand;
   one of his heralds,
        yes, I would sing
   loudest hosannas! Jesus is king.

Meter: 8 4 8 4 5 4 5 4

Words: William H. Parker, 1885

Amazing Grace 72

1. Amazing grace, how sweet the sound,
   that saved a wretch like me!
   I once was lost, but now am found,
   was blind, but now I see.

2. 'Twas grace that taught my heart
         to fear,
   and grace my fears relieved;
   how precious did that grace appear
   the hour I first believed.

3. Thro' many dangers, toils,
         and snares,
   I have already come;
   'tis grace that brought me safe
         thus far,
   and grace will lead me home.

4. The Lord has promised good to me,
   this word my hope secures;
   God will my shield and portion be
   as long as life endures.

Meter: CM

Words: John Newton, 1779, rev.

73 God of Grace and God of Glory

1. God of grace and God of glory,
   on thy people pour thy power;
   crown thine ancient church's story;
   bring her bud to glorious flower.
   Grant us wisdom, grant us courage,
   for the facing of this hour.

2. Lo! the hosts of evil round us
   scorn thy Christ, assail his ways!
   Fears and doubts too long have
         bound us;
   free our hearts to work and praise.
   Grant us wisdom, grant us courage,
   for the living of these days.

3. Save us from weak resignation
   to the evils we deplore;
   let the search for thy salvation
   be our glory evermore.
   Grant us wisdom, grant us courage,
   serving thee whom we adore.

Meter: 8 7 8 7 8 7

Words: Harry Emerson Fosdick, 1930
Used by permission of Elinor Fosdick Downs.

Jesus Bids Us Shine 74

1. Jesus bids us shine
     with a pure, clear light,
   Like a little candle
     burning in the night.
   In this world is darkness;
     so let us shine,
   You in your small corner,
     and I in mine.

2. Jesus bids us shine,
     first of all for him;
   Well he sees and knows it,
     if our light grows dim:
   He looks down from heaven
     to see us shine,
   You in your small corner,
     and I in mine.

3. Jesus bids us shine,
     then, for all around;
   Many kinds of darkness
     in the world are found—
   Sin, and want, and sorrow;
     so we must shine,
   You in your small corner,
     and I in mine.

Meter: 5 5 6 5 6 4 6 4

Words: Susan Warner, 1819–1885

75   Here I Am, Lord

1. I, the Lord of sea and sky,
   I have heard my people cry.
   All who dwell in dark and sin
       my hand will save.
   I who made the stars of night,
   I will make their darkness bright.
   Who will bear my light to them?
       Whom shall I send?

   Refrain:
   Here I am, Lord. Is it I, Lord?
   I have heard you calling
       in the night.
   I will go, Lord, if you lead me.
   I will hold your people
       in my heart.

2. I, the Lord of snow and rain,
   I have borne my people's pain.
   I have wept for love of them.
       They turn away.
   I will break their hearts of stone,
   give them hearts for love alone.
   I will speak my word to them.
       Whom shall I send?

3. I, the Lord of wind and flame,
   I will tend the poor and lame,
   I will set a feast for them.
        My hand will save.
   Finest bread I will provide
   till their hearts be satisfied.
   I will give my life to them.
        Whom shall I send?

Meter: 7 7 7 4 D with refrain

Words: Daniel L. Schutte, SJ, 1981

76 How Firm a Foundation

1. How firm a foundation,
        ye saints of the Lord,
    is laid for your faith
        in his excellent word!
    What more can he say
        than to you he hath said,
    to you who to Jesus
        for refuge have fled?

2. 'Fear not, I am with thee;
        O be not dismayed!
    For I am thy God
        and will still give thee aid;
    I'll strengthen thee, help thee,
        and cause thee to stand,
    upheld by my righteous
        omnipotent hand.

3. 'When through the deep waters
        I call thee to go,
    the rivers of woe
        shall not thee overflow;
    for I will be with thee,
        thy troubles to bless,
    and sanctify to thee
        thy deepest distress.

4. 'When through fiery trials
    thy pathway shall lie,
my grace, all-sufficient,
    shall be thy supply:
the flame shall not hurt thee;
    I only design
thy dross to consume,
    and thy gold to refine.

5. The soul that on Jesus
    hath leaned for repose
I will not—I will not
    desert to his foes;
that soul, though all hell
    should endeavor to shake,
I'll never—no, never—
    no, never forsake!'

Meter: 11 11 11 11

Words: R. Keen, C. 1787

77 Jesus Calls Us; O'er the Tumult

1. Jesus calls us; o'er the tumult
   of our life's wild restless sea,
   day by day his sweet voice soundeth,
   saying, 'Christian, follow me,'

2. As of old Saint Andrew heard it
   by the Galilean lake,
   turned from home and toil
       and kindred,
   leaving all for his dear sake.

3. Jesus calls us from the worship
   of the vain world's golden store,
   from each idol that would keep us,
   saying, 'Christian, love me more.'

4. In our joys and in our sorrows,
   days of toil and hours of ease,
   still he calls, in cares and pleasures,
   'Christian, love me more than these.'

5. Jesus calls us: by thy mercies,
   Savior, may we hear thy call,
   give our hearts to thine obedience,
   serve and love thee best of all.

Meter: 8 7 8 7

Words: Cecil Frances Alexander, 1818–1895

Just As I Am, Without One Plea

78

1. Just as I am, without one plea,
   but that thy blood was shed for me,
   and that thou bidst me come to thee,
   O Lamb of God, I come, I come.

2. Just as I am, though tossed about
   with many a conflict, many a doubt,
   fightings and fears within, without,
   O Lamb of God, I come, I come.

3. Just as I am, thou wilt receive,
   wilt welcome, pardon, cleanse,
      relieve;
   because thy promise I believe,
   O Lamb of God, I come, I come.

4. Just as I am, thy love unknown
   hath broken every barrier down;
   now, to be thine, yea, thine alone,
   O Lamb of God, I come, I come.

Meter: 8 8 8 8

Words: Charlotte Elliott, 1835

79 O Jesus, I Have Promised

1. O Jesus, I have promised
      to serve thee to the end;
   be thou for ever near me,
      my master and my friend:
   I shall not fear the battle
      if thou art by my side,
   nor wander from the pathway
      if thou wilt be my guide.

2. O let me hear thee speaking
      in accents clear and still,
   above the storms of passion,
      the murmurs of self-will;
   O speak to reassure me,
      to hasten or control;
   O speak, and make me listen,
      thou guardian of my soul.

3. O Jesus, thou hast promised
      to all who follow thee,
   that where thou art in glory
      there shall thy servant be;
   and Jesus, I have promised
      to serve thee to the end;
   O give me grace to follow,
      my master and my friend.

Meter: 7 6 7 6 D

Words: John Ernest Bode, 1816–1874

O Master, Let Me Walk with Thee 80

1. O Master, let me walk with thee
in lowly paths of service free;
teach me thy secret, help me bear
the strain of toil, the fret of care.

2. Help me the slow of heart to move
with some clear, winning word
    of love;
teach me the wayward feet to stay,
and guide them in the
    homeward way.

3. Teach me thy patience; still
    with thee,
in closer, dearer company,
in work that keeps faith sweet
    and strong,
in trust that triumphs over wrong,

4. In hope that sends a shining ray
far down the future's
    broadening way,
in peace that only thou canst give,
with thee, O Master, let me live.

Meter: 8 8 8 8

Words: Washington Gladden, 1836–1918

81 One More Step

1. One more step along the world I go.
   One more step along the world I go.
   From the old things to the new
   keep me traveling along with you.

   Refrain:
   And it's from the old I travel
       to the new.
   Keep me traveling along with you.

2. Round the corner of the world I turn.
   More and more about the world
       I learn.
   All the new things that I see
   you'll be looking at along with me.

3. As I travel through the bad and good
   Keep me traveling the way I should.
   Where I see no way to go
   You'll be telling me the way, I know.

4. Give me courage when the world
      is rough.
   Keep me loving though the world
      is tough.
   Leap and sing in all I do.
   Keep me traveling along with you.

5. You are older than the world can be.
   You are younger than the life in me.
   Ever old and ever new.
   Keep me traveling along with you.

Meter: irregular

Words: Sydney Carter

82 Open My Eyes That I May See

1. Open my eyes that I may see
   glimpses of truth thou hast for me;
   place in my hands the wonderful key
   that shall unclasp and set me free.

   Refrain:
   Silently now I wait for thee,
   　　ready, my God, thy will to see;
   open my eyes, illumine me,
   　　Spirit divine!

2. Open my ears that I may hear
   voices of truth thou sendest clear,
   and while the wavenotes fall
   　　on my ear,
   ev'rything false will disappear.

3. Open my mouth and let me bear
   gladly the warm truth ev'rywhere;
   open my heart and let me prepare
   love with thy children thus to share.

Meter: 8 8 9 8 with refrain

Words: Clara H. Scott, 1895

Seek Ye First the Kingdom of God 83

1. Seek ye first the kingdom of God,
   and God's righteousness
   and all these things shall be added
   unto you. Allelu, alleluia.

2. We do not live by bread alone,
   but by ev'ry word
   that proceeds from the mouth
   of God. Allelu, alleluia.

3. Ask and it shall be given unto you;
   seek and you shall find;
   knock and the door shall be opened
   unto you. Allelu, alleluia.

Meter: irregular

84 Take My Life and Let It Be

1. Take my life and let it be
   consecrated, Lord, to thee;
   take my moments and my days,
   let them flow in ceaseless praise.

2. Take my hands, and let them move
   at the impulse of thy love;
   take my feet, and let them be
   swift and purposeful for thee.

3. Take my lips and let them be
   filled with messages from thee;
   take my intellect, and use
   every power as thou shalt choose.

4. Take my will, and make it thine;
   it shall be no longer mine;
   take my heart, it is thine own;
   it shall be thy royal throne.

5. Take my love: my Lord, I pour
   at thy feet its treasure store;
   take myself, and I will be,
   ever, only, all for thee.

Meter: 7 7 7 7

Words: Frances Ridley Havergal, 1836–1879

Blest Be the Tie That Binds   85

1. Blest be the tie that binds
   our hearts in Christian love;
   the unity of heart and mind
   is like to that above.

2. Before our Maker's throne
   we pour our ardent prayers;
   our fears, our hopes, our aims
      are one,
   our comforts and our cares.

3. We share each other's woes,
   each other's burdens bear;
   and often for each other flows
   the sympathising tear.

4. This glorious hope revives
   our courage on the way;
   that we shall live in perfect love
   in God's eternal day.

Meter: 6 6 8 6

Words: John Fawcett, 1782

86 The Servant Song

1. Sister, let me be your servant,
   let me be as Christ to you;
   pray that I may have the grace to
   let you be my servant too.

2. We are pilgrims on a journey,
   fellow trav'lers on the road;
   we are here to help each other
   walk the mile and bear the load.

3. I will hold the Chirst-light for you
   in the night time of your fear;
   I will hold my hand out to you,
   speak the peace you long to hear.

4. I will weep when you are weeping,
   when you laugh I'll laugh with you;
   I will share your joy and sorrow,
   till we've seen this journey thro'.

5. When we sing to God in heaven,
   we shall find such harmony,
   born of all we've known together
   of Christ's love and agony.

6.   Brother, let me be your servant,
     let me be as Christ to you;
     pray that I may have the grace to
     let you be my servant too.

Meter: 8 7 8 7

What Does the Lord Require of You?   87

What does the Lord require of you?
Justice, kindness, walk humbly
     with your God.
To seek justice and love kindness
     and walk humbly with your God.

Meter: irregular

88   For the Healing of the Nations

1. For the healing of the nations,
   God, we pray with one accord;
   for a just and equal sharing
   of the things that earth affords.
   To a life of love in action
   help us rise and pledge our word.

2. Lead us, Father, into freedom
   from despair your world release;
   that, redeemed from war
        and hatred,
   all may come and go in peace.
   Show us how thro' care
        and goodness
   fear will die and hope increase.

3. All that kills abundant living,
   let it from the earth be banned:
   pride of status, race or schooling,
   dogmas that obscure your plan.
   In our common quest for justice
   may we hallow life's brief span.

4. You, Creator God have written
    your great name on humankind;
    for our growing in your likeness,
    bring the life of Christ to mind;
    that by our response and service
    earth its destiny may find.

Meter: 8 7 8 7 8 7

Words: Fred Kaan, 1965
Copyright © 1968 by Hope Publishing, Co., Carol Stream,
IL 60188. All rights reserved. Used by permission.

89 Community of Christ

1. Community of Christ,
   who make the Cross your own,
   live out your creed and risk
       your life for God alone:
   the God who wears your face,
   to whom all worlds belong,
   whose children are of every
       race and every song.

2. Community of Christ,
   look past the Church's door
   and see the refugee,
       the hungry, and the poor.
   Take hands with the oppressed,
   the jobless in your street,
   take towel and water, that you
       wash your neighbor's feet.

3. Community of Christ,
   through whom the word
         must sound—
   cry out for justice and for peace
         the whole world round:
   disarm the powers that war
   and all that can destroy,
   turn bombs to bread,
         and tears of anguish into joy.

4. When menace melts away,
   so shall God's will be done,
   the climate of the world
         be peace and Christ its Sun;
   our currency be love
   and kindliness our law,
   our food and faith be shared as
         one for evermore.

Meter: 6 6 8 4 D

Words: Shirley Erena Murray

90 Help Us Accept Each Other

1. Help us accept each other
       as Christ accepted us;
   teach us as sister, brother,
       each person to embrace.
   Be present, God, among us
       and bring us to believe
   we are ourselves accepted
       and meant to love and live.

2. Teach us, O God, your lessons,
       as in our daily life
   we struggle to be human
       and search for hope and faith.
   Teach us to care for people,
       for all—not just for some,
   to love them as we find them
       or as they may become.

3. Lord, for today's encounters
       with all who are in need,
   who hunger for acceptance,
       for righteousness and bread,
   we need new eyes for seeing,
       new hands for holding on:
   renew us with your Spirit;
       come, free us, make us one!

Meter: 7 6 7 6 D

Words: Fred Kaan, 1974

Rise Up, O Saints of God 91

1. Rise up, O saints of God!
    From vain ambitions turn;
    Christ rose triumphant that
        your hearts
    with nobler zeal might burn.

2. Speak out, O saints of God!
    Despair engulfs earth's frame;
    as heirs of God's baptismal grace
    the word of hope proclaim.

3. Rise up, O saints of God!
    The kingdom's task embrace;
    redress sin's cruel consequence;
    give justice larger place.

4. Give heed, O saints of God!
    Creation cries in pain;
    stretch forth your hand of
        healing now,
    with love the weak sustain.

5   Commit your hearts to seek
    the path which Christ has trod,
    and, quickened by the Spirit's power,
    rise up, O saints of God!

Meter: 6 6 8 6

Words: Norman O. Forness, 1977
Copyright © Norman O. Forness. Used by permission.

92 Let There Be Light

1. Let there be light,
    let there be understanding,
    let all the nations gather,
    let them be face to face;

2. Open our lips,
    open our minds to ponder,
    open the door of concord
    opening into grace;

3. Perish the sword,
    perish the angry judgement,
    perish the bombs and hunger,
    perish the fight for gain;

4. Hallow our love,
    hallow the deaths of martyrs,
    hallow their holy freedom,
    hallowed be thy name;

5. Thy kingdom come,
   thy spirit turn to language,
   thy people speak together,
   thy spirit never fade;

6. Let there be light,
   open our hearts to wonder,
   perish the way of terror,
   hallow the world God made.

Meter: 4 7 7 6

93 I Am the Light of the World

Refrain:
'I am the light of the world!
You people come and follow me!'
If you follow and love
you'll learn the mystery
of what you were meant to do and be.

1. When the song of the angels
        is stilled,
   when the star in the sky
        is gone,
   when the kings and the shepherds
   have found their way home,
   the work of Christmas is begun:

2. To find the lost and lonely one,
   to heal the broken soul
        with love,
   to feed the hungry children
        with warmth and good food,
   to feel the earth below
        the sky above!

3. To free the pris'ner from
       all chains,
   to make the powerful care,
   to rebuild the nations
   with strength of good will,
   to see God's children
       ev'rywhere!

4. To bring hope to ev'ry task
       you do,
   To dance at a baby's new birth,
   To make music in
       an old person's heart,
   And sing to the colors
       of the earth!

Meter: irregular

Words: Jim Strathdee, 1969
Copyright © 1969 by Desert Flower Music,
Carmichael, CA 95609
Used by permission.

94   Part of the Family

Refrain:
Come in, come in and sit down
you are a part of the fam'ly.
We are lost and we are found,
and we are a part of the fam'ly.

1. You know the reason
        why you came,
    yet no reason can explain;
    so share in the laughter and cry
        in the pain,
    for we are a part of the fam'ly.
    God is with us in this place,
    like a mother's warm embrace.
    We're all forgiven by God's grace,
    for we are a part of the fam'ly.

2. Children and elders, middlers
        and teens,
    singles and doubles and
        in-betweens,
    strong eighty-fivers and
        streetwise sixteens,
    for we are a part of the fam'ly.

Greeters and shoppers,
    long-time and new,
nobody here has a claim on a pew;
and whether we're many
    or whether we're few,
we are a part of the fam'ly.

3.   There's life to be shared
    in the bread and the wine;
we are the branches,
    Christ is the vine.
This is God's temple,
    it's not yours or mine,
but we are a part of the fam'ly.
There's rest for the weary
    and health for us all;
there's a yoke that is easy,
    and a burden that's small.
So come in and worship
    and answer the call,
for we are a part of the fam'ly.

Meter: irregular

95 To Show by Touch and Word

1. To show by touch and word
       devotion to the earth,
   to hold in full regard
       all life that comes to birth,
   we need, O God, the will to find
   the good you had of old in mind.

2. Renew our minds to choose
       the things that matter most,
   our hearts to long for truth
       till pride of self is lost.
   For ev'ry challenge that we face
   we need your guidance and
       your grace.

3. Let love from day to day
       be yardstick, rule and norm,
   and let our lives portray
       your word in human form.
   Now come with us that we
       may have
   your wits about us where
       we live.

Meter: 6 6 6 6 8 8

Words: Fred Kaan, 1974
Copyright © 1975 by Hope Publishing, Co., Carol Stream,
IL 60188. All rights reserved. Used by permission.

We Are the Church 96

Refrain:
I am the church! You are the church!
We are the church together!
All who follow Jesus,
    all around the world!
Yes, we're the church together.

1. The church is not a building,
   the church is not a steeple,
   the church is not a resting place,
   the church is a people!

2. We're many kinds of people
   with many kinds of faces,
   all colors and all ages, too,
   from all times and places.

3. At Pentecost some people
   received the Holy Spirit
   and told the Good News through the
   world to all who would hear it.

4. I count if I am ninety,
   or nine, or just a baby;
   there's one thing I am sure about
   and I don't mean maybe:

Meter: irregular

Words: Richard Avery & Donald Marsh, 1972
Copyright © 1972 by Hope Publishing, Co., Carol Stream,
IL 60188. All rights reserved. Used by permission.

97 Walls That Divide

1. Tho' ancient walls may still
        stand proud
   and racial strife be fact,
   tho' bound'ries may be lines
        of hate,
   proclaim God's saving act!

   Refrain:
   Walls that divide are broken down;
   Christ is our unity!
   Chains that enslave are
        thrown aside;
   Christ is our liberty!

2. When vested pow'r stands
        firm entrenched
   and breaks another's back,
   when waste and want live side
        by side,
   it's gospel that we lack!

3. The truth we seek in
        varied scheme,
   the life that we pursue,
   unites us in a common quest
   for self and world made new!

4. The church divided seeks
     that grace,
that newness we proclaim;
a unity of serving love
that lives to praise God's name!

5. This broken world seeks
     lasting health
and vital unity—
God's people in the Christ
     made new
cast off all slavery!

Meter: 8 6 8 6 with refrain

Words: Walter Farquharson, 1974

98 Prayer of St. Francis

1. Make me a channel of your peace:
   where there is hatred, let me bring
      your love;
   where there is injury, your healing
      pow'r,
   and where there's doubt, true faith
      in you.

2. Make me a channel of your peace:
   where there's despair in life let me
      bring hope;
   where there is darkness, only light,
   and where there's sadness, ever joy.

3. O Spirit, grant that I may never seek
   so much to be consoled as to console,
   to be understood as to understand,
   to be loved as to love with all my soul.

4. Make me a channel of your peace.
   It is in pardoning that we are
      pardoned,
   in giving to all that we receive,
   and in dying that we're born to
      eternal life.

Meter: irregular

Words: Traditional

Let There Be Peace on Earth

99

1. Let there be peace on earth
       and let it begin with me;
   let there be peace on earth,
       the peace that was meant to be.
   With God, our creator,
       children all are we;
   let us walk with each other
       in perfect harmony.

2. Let peace begin with me,
       let this be the moment now,
   with ev'ry step I take
       let this be my solemn vow:
   to take each moment and
       live each moment in peace
       eternally.
   Let there be peace on earth
       and let it begin with me.

Meter: irregular

100 Come and Find the Quiet Center

1. Come and find the quiet center
   in the crowded life we lead,
   find the room for hope to enter,
   find the frame where we are freed:
   clear the chaos and the clutter,
   clear our eyes, that we can see
   all the things that really matter,
   be at peace, and simply be.

2. Silence is a friend who claims us,
   cools the heat and slows the pace,
   God it is who speaks and names us,
   knows our being, touches base,
   making space within our thinking,
   lifting shades to show the sun,
   raising courage when we're shrinking,
   finding scope for faith begun.

3. In the Spirit let us travel,
   open to each other's pain,
   let our loves and fears unravel,
   celebrate the space we gain:
   there's a place for deepest dreaming,
   there's a time for heart to care,
   in the Spirit's lively scheming
   there is always room to spare!

Meter: 8 7 8 7 D

There Is a Balm in Gilead 101

Refrain:
There is a balm in Gilead
    to make the wounded whole.
There is a balm in Gilead
    to heal the sin-sick soul.

1. Sometimes I feel discouraged,
and think my work's in vain,
but then the Holy Spirit
revives my soul again.

2. Don't ever feel discouraged,
for Jesus is your friend,
and if you lack for knowledge
he'll not refuse to lend.

3. If you cannot preach like Peter,
if you cannot pray like Paul,
you can tell the love of Jesus
and say, 'He died for all.'

Meter: 7 6 7 6 with refrain

African-American Spiritual

102 Be Still, My Soul

1. Be still, my soul:
      the Lord is on your side.
   Bear patiently
      the cross of grief or pain;
   leave to your God
      to order and provide;
   in every change
      God faithful will remain.
   Be still, my soul:
      your best, your heavenly friend
   through thorny ways
      leads to a joyful end.

2. Be still, my soul:
      your God will undertake
   to guide the future,
      as in ages past.
   Your hope, your confidence
      let nothing shake;
   all now mysterious
      shall be bright at last.
   Be still, my soul:
      the waves and winds still know
   the Christ who ruled them
      while he dwelt below.

3. Be still, my soul:
   the hour is hastening on
when we shall be
   forever with the Lord,
when disappointment,
   grief, and fear are gone,
sorrow forgot,
   love's purest joys restored.
Be still, my soul:
   when change and tears are past,
all safe and blessed
   we shall meet at last.

Meter: 11 10 11 10 11 10

Words: Katharina von Schlegel, 1752
tr. Jane Borthwick, 1855

It's Me, O Lord 103

Refrain:
It's me, it's me, O Lord,
   standing in the need of prayer.

1. Not my brother, not my sister,

2. Not the preacher, not the deacon,

3. Not my father, not my mother,

Meter: irregular
African-American Spiritual

104 Be Thou My Vision

1. Be thou my vision,
    O Lord of my heart;
   naught be all else to me
    save that thou art,
   thou my best thought,
    by day or by night,
   waking or sleeping
    thy presence my light.

2. Be thou my wisdom,
    thou my true word;
   I ever with thee,
    thou with me, Lord;
   thou my great Father,
    I thy true Son,
   thou in me dwelling,
    and I with thee one.

3. High King of heaven,
    after victory won,
   may I reach heaven's joys,
    O bright heaven's sun!
   Heart of my own heart,
    whatever befall,
   still be my vision,
    O ruler of all.

Meter: 10 10 10 10

Words: 8th C. Irish
tr. Mary Byrne, 1880–1931 & Eleanor Hull, 1860–1935

What a Friend We Have in Jesus 105

1. What a friend we have in Jesus,
all our sins and griefs to bear!
What a privilege to carry
everything to God in prayer!
O what peace we often forfeit,
O what needless pain we bear,
all because we do not carry
everything to God in prayer!

2. Have we trials or temptations?
Is there trouble anywhere?
We should never be discouraged;
take it to the Lord in prayer.
Can we find a friend so faithful,
who will all our sorrows share?
Jesus knows our every weakness;
take it to the Lord in prayer.

3. Are we weak and heavy-laden,
cumbered with a load of care?
Christ the Savior is our refuge;
take it to the Lord in prayer.
Do thy friends despise, forsake us?
Are we tempted to despair?
Jesus' strength will shield
    our weakness,
and we'll find new courage there.

Meter: 8 7 8 7 D

Words: Joseph M. Scriven, c. 1855

106 Take Time to Be Holy

1. Take time to be holy,
      speak oft with thy Lord;
   abide in him always,
      and feed on his word.
   Make friends of God's children,
      help those who are weak,
   forgetting in nothing
      his blessing to seek.

2. Take time to be holy,
      the world rushes on;
   spend much time in secret
      with Jesus alone.
   By looking to Jesus,
      like him thou shalt be;
   thy friends in thy conduct
      his likeness shall see.

3. Take time to be holy,
      let him be thy guide,
   and run not before him,
      whatever betide.
   In joy or in sorrow,
      still follow the Lord,
   and, looking to Jesus,
      still trust in his word.

4. Take time to be holy,
   be calm in thy soul,
   each thought and each motive
   beneath his control.
   Thus led by his spirit
   to fountains of love,
   thou soon shalt be fitted
   for service above.

Meter: 6 5 6 5 D

Words: William D. Longstaff, c. 1882

Kum Ba Yah 107

1. Kum ba yah, my Lord,
   Kum ba yah!
   O Lord, Kum ba yah!

2. Someone's crying Lord,

3. Someone's praying, Lord,

4. Someone's singing, Lord,

5. Come by here, my Lord,
   Come by here!

Meter: irregular

Traditional

108 Abide with Me

1. Abide with me;
        fast falls the eventide;
   the darkness deepens;
        Lord, with me abide;
   when other helpers fail,
        and comforts flee,
   help of the helpless,
        O abide with me.

2. Swift to its close
        ebbs out life's little day;
   earth's joys grow dim,
        its glories pass away;
   change and decay
        in all around I see;
   O thou who changest not,
        abide with me.

3. I need thy presence
        every passing hour;
   what but thy grace
        can foil the tempter's power?
   Who like thyself
        my guide and stay can be?
   Through cloud and sunshine,
        Lord, abide with me.

4. I fear no foe
       with thee at hand to bless;
   ills have no weight,
       and tears no bitterness.
   Where is death's sting?
       Where, grave, thy victory?
   I triumph still,
       if thou abide with me.

5. Hold thou thy cross
       before my closing eyes;
   shine through the gloom,
       and point me to the skies;
   heaven's morning breaks,
       and earth's vain shadows flee:
   in life, in death,
       O Lord, abide with me.

Meter: 10 10 10 10

Words: Henry Francis Lyte, 1793–1847

109 The Day Thou Gavest

1. The day thou gavest, Lord, is ended;
   the darkness falls at thy behest;
   to thee our morning hymns
       ascended,
   thy praise shall sanctify our rest.

2. We thank thee that thy church
       unsleeping,
   while earth rolls onward into light,
   through all the world her watch is
       keeping,
   and rests not now by day or night.

3. As o'er each continent and island
   the dawn leads on another day,
   the voice of prayer is never silent,
   nor dies the strain of praise away.

4. So be it, Lord! Thy throne shall
       never,
   like earth's proud empires, pass
       away;
   thy kingdom stands, and grows
       for ever,
   till all thy creatures own thy sway.

Meter: 9 8 9 8

Words: John Ellerton, 1826–1893

Now the Day Is Over 110

1. Now the day is over,
   night is drawing nigh,
   shadows of the evening
   steal across the sky.

2. Jesus, give the weary
   calm and sweet repose;
   with thy tenderest blessing
   may mine eyelids close.

3. Comfort those who suffer,
   watching late in pain;
   those who plan some evil
   from their sin restrain.

4. When the morning wakens,
   then may I arise
   pure, and fresh, and sinless
   in thy holy eyes.

Meter: 6 5 6 5

Words: Sabine Baring-Gould, 1865, rev.

Go Now in Peace 111

Go now in peace, go now in peace.
May the love of God surround you
ev'rywhere, ev'rywhere you may go.

Meter: irregular

Words: Natalie Sleeth, 1976

Addresses of Copyright Holders

Copyright Company
40 Music Square E
Nashville, TN 37203

David Higham Associates
5–8 Lower John Street
Golden Square,
London W1R 4HA

Davis, Frances
5205 Belmore Avenue
Montreal, QC H4V 2C7

Desert Flower Music
Box 1476
Carmichael, CA 95609

Downs, Elinor Fosdick
63 Altantic Avenue
Boston, MA 02110

EMI Christian Music Group
PO Box 5085
101 Winners Circle
Brentwood, TN 37024–5085

Estate of John S. Rice
10619 Alameda Drive
Knoxville, TN 37932

Farquharson, Walter H.
Box 126
Saltcoats, SK S0A 3R0

Forness, Norman O.
38 East Stevens Street
Gettysburg, PA 17325

Frederick Harris Music
529 Speers Road
Oakville, ON L6K 2G4

Hinshaw Music Inc.
PO Box 470
Chapel Hill, NC 27514–0470

Hope Publishing Company
380 South Main Place
Carol Stream, IL 60188

Jan-Lee Music
c/o Janet Taché
PO Box 1517
Honokaa, HI 96727

Manley, James K.
434 Ives Terrace
Sunnyvale, CA 94087

Manna Music Inc.
35255 Brooten Road
Pacific City, OR 97135

McGuire, Cherie
87 Cardinal Crescent
Chatham, ON N7L 3V4

New Dawn Music
PO Box 13248
Portland, OR 97213

OCP Publications
5536 NE Hassalo
Portland, OR 97213

Songs for a Gospel People
c/o Wood Lake Books
10162 Newene Road
Winfield, BC V4V 1R2

Table of Contents

(Title is in italics when it differs from the first line)